About to Disappear

About to Disappear

Robbi Nester

SHANTI ARTS PUBLISHING

BRUNSWICK, MAINE

A special thank you to those who have supported, encouraged, and helped me to put this and other ekphrastic work together and get it out into the world. I am so grateful to Dean Rader for giving me a new and larger perspective on making ekphrastic manuscripts; Lorette C. Luzajic for introducing me to the community of ekphrastic writers and encouraging me to discover art that was new to me; Clare MacQueen for publishing and supporting my work and believing in it when others did not; Marjorie Maddox for being a friend and supporter as well as giving me new ideas about the directions in which ekphrastic writing could be taken; Marley Youmans, who has been doing beautiful ekphrastic writing for as long as I can remember; and John Brantingham, a friend and teacher for many years who has spoken about my work to anyone who would listen. Also, thank you to the many artists who have collaborated with and inspired me, allowing me to publish their images with my poems. And to my husband, Richard Nester, for his support and willingness to listen. It takes a village.

Contents

Law of Attraction

Ad Nihilum

Images

[45]   Grant Wood, *American Gothic*, 1930. Oil on beaverboard. 30.7 x 25.7 inches (78 x 65.3 cm). Art Institute of Chicago. Wikimedia Commons. Public Domain.

[46]   Vincent van Gogh, *Three White Cottages in Saintes-Maries*, 1888. Oil on canvas. 13.1 x 16.3 inches (33.5 x 41.5 cm). Kunsthaus Zürich, Switzerland. Wikimedia Commons. Public Domain.

[49]   Robert Rhodes, *Winter: Farm Land, Lancaster County*, 2020. Used with permission.

[51]   Sallie Swift, *Evolving Sirenian*, 2012. Used with permission.

[52]   nasa / YjiM5riCKk4 / unsplash.com

[55]   Rupert Jessup, *Fitting*. Used with permission.

[59]   Kylli Sparre, *Disquiet*, 2019. Used with permission.

[63]   Aggie Zed, *Magician*, 2001. Used with permission.

[65]   Nick Brandt, *Petrified Flamingo, Lake Natron*, 2013. Used with permission.

[66]   Sally Gall, *Heavenly Creatures #2*. Used with permission.

[71]   Vincent van Gogh, *Starry Night on the Rhone*, 1888. Oil on canvas. 28.3 x 36.2 inches (72 x 92 cm). Musée d'Orsay, Paris, France. Wikimedia Commons. Public Domain.

[73]   Magan Ruthke, *Wisdom in the Missouri*, 2017. Used with permission.

[76]   Edward Hopper, *Nighthawks*, 1942. Oil on canvas. 33.1 x 60 inches (84.1 x 152.4 cm). Art Institute of Chicago. Wikimedia Commons. Public Domain.

[79]   Johannes Vermeer, *Girl Interrupted at Her Music*, c. 1658–61. Oil on canvas. 15.5 x 17.5 inches (39.4 x 44.5 cm). The Frick Collection, New York City. Wikimedia Commons. Public Domain.

[81]   John Singer Sargent, *El Jaleo*, 1882. Oil on canvas. 91.3 x 136.8 inches (232 x 348 cm). Isabella Stewart Gardner Museum, Boston, Massachusetts. Wikimedia Commons. Public Domain.

[83]   Robert Rhodes, *Fog and Moonlight: Margaret in her Nightgown, Alone in Bella's Yard*, 2023. Used with permission.

[84]   Vincent van Gogh, *The Night Café*, 1888. Oil on canvas. 28.5 x 36.2 inches (72.4 x 92.1 cm). Yale University Art Gallery, New Haven, Connecticut. Wikimedia Commons. Public Domain.

[91]   Holly Wilmuth, *The Iguana or Benevolent Dragon*, 2014. Used with permission. www.hollywilmeth.com

[95]   J. M. W. Turner, *The Burning of the Houses of Lords and Commons, 16 October 1934*, 1834. Oil on canvas. 36.2 x 48.4 inches (92 x 123 cm). Cleveland Museum of Art. Wikimedia Commons. Public Domain.

[96]   Edward Hopper, *Gas*, 1940. Oil on canvas. 26.2 x 40.2 inches (66.6 x 102.2 cm). Museum of Modern Art, New York City. Wikimedia Commons. Public Domain.

[101] Oceola Refetoff, *Bruce and Elsie, Independence, CA*. Used with permission.

[105] Daniel Mauermann, *Pierced Man*, 2008. Used with permission.

[107] Josef Capek, *Piják*, 1918–19. Private collection. Wikimedia Commons. Public Domain.

Acknowledgments

The author extends her gratitude to the editors of the following publication in which these poems first appeared:

Aeolian Harp, Vol. VI: "Woman with Iguanas"

Artemis: "Night Painting" and "Peasant Wedding"

Cultural Weekly: "After Veils"

Dark Ink (Moon Tide Press, ed. Eric Morago): "Sea Star"

Ekphrastic Review: "After Pharmacy"; "After Three White Cottages at Saintes-Maries"; "El Jaleo"; "Evolving Sirenian"; "Girl Interrupted at her Music"; "Gogol's Dream"; "In the Balance"; "Law of Attraction"; "Night Hawks"; and "Title Unspecified"

Free State Review: "Love Letter to the Sky"

Gyroscope Review: "Ark"

The Hummingbird Review: "Looking at Jupiter"

Imposter: "Man Smoking"

The Light Ekphrastic: "The Lives of Rivers"

MacQueen's Quinterly: "Book"; "Dangerous Dreams"; "On Adaptation"; "Summer Sheltering in Place"; "Under the Metal"; and "Watching Pins"

Negative Capability: "Disquiet" and "Her Complaint"

Peacock Journal: "Fog and Moonlight"

Poemeleon: "Avenue of Oaks"; "Dragon's Blood Trees"; "Momento Mütter"; and "Once a Raven"

Poets Facing the Wall: "Ghost Wall and "The Wall"

Rise Up Review: "Family Portrait with Guns"

SoFloPoMo: "The Harem Speaks"

SWWIM: "October is Burning"

Verse-Virtual: "On a Leonardo Drawing"

Visual Verse: "American Gothic"; "Creation Story"; "Fitting"; "Sea Bed"; and "Two Ways of Taking Up Space"

Ex Nihilo

Some Assembly Required

—after Sal Taylor Kydd, *Watching Pins*

The mind is always brewing something,
tracing shape-shifting menageries in clouds.
Any plain ingredients—flour, water,
and a bit of yeast and salt, plus time,
can rise to the occasion, becoming
a new thing. So a handful of steel pins
dropped on a table spurs the mind
to summon forces far beyond itself,
as sages once scanned the entrails
of a bird, thrown sticks, or tea leaves
at the bottom of a cup for wisdom
that could change a nation or affect
a life. What emerges depends upon
the mind at work. Maybe a strategy
to solve a city's traffic woes, a way
to plan political maneuvers or a play
in sports. Philosophy and science
are full of sudden insights of this sort,
like Newton's apple, Archimedes
bending over water rising in a tub.
The chemist August Kekule learned
the Benzine atom's structure
from the sudden vision of a snake
swallowing its tail. In the pandemic,
when the rules of ordinary life were
all suspended and time became the most
plentiful commodity, we could stare at nothing,
like a cat intent on tracking birds outside
the window. People looked back on their lives,

hoping to mend old rifts, contacting former friends or enemies, the quarrels long forgotten. We changed, like dough rising at the back of a warm stove. Sequestered in our homes, we braided our loose threads into a pattern, wrote plays, made a family, discovered special gifts we didn't know we had, found power at the tips of our own fingers.

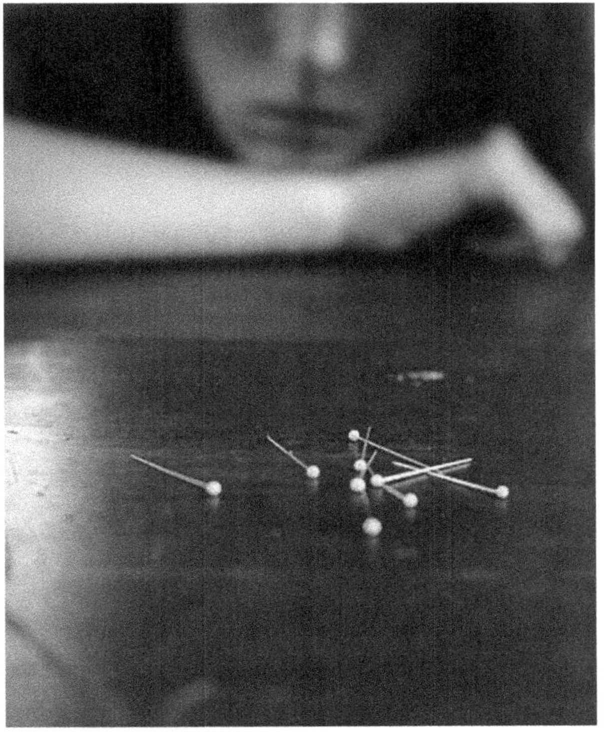

Sal Taylor Kydd, *Watching Pins*, 2015

Book

—after Maggy Jaszczak, *untitled hand fan*

Toss a pebble in the still pond, and watch
the spot swell and spread, becoming
the petals of a sunflower, wide eye
edged with lashes curling at the tip.
That's what happens each time
you open a book, the world growing
larger with each page, silent ciphers
sprouting cities and roads, and finally,
a Ferris wheel, sending its iron tendrils
into the air, where you sit, slowly swaying
in your seat, looking out onto the new-made world.

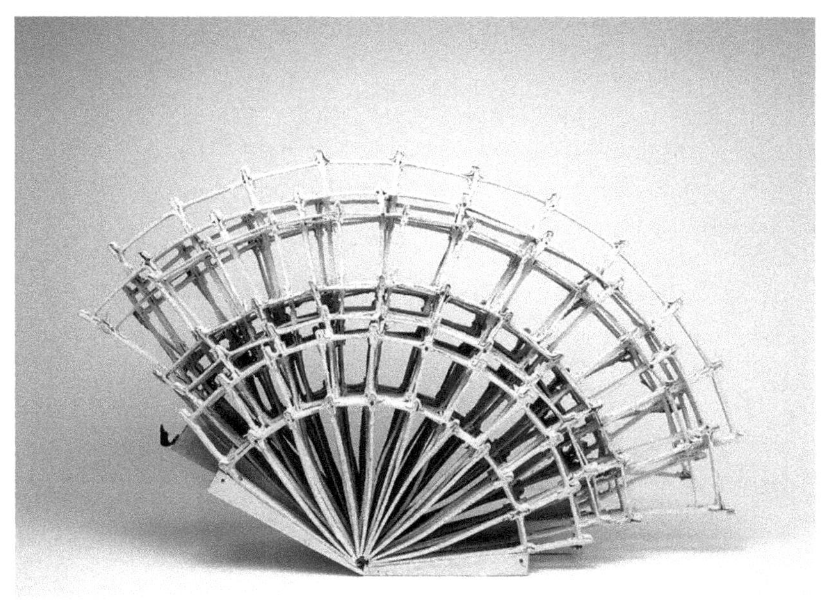

Maggy Jaszczak, *untitled hand fan,* 2018

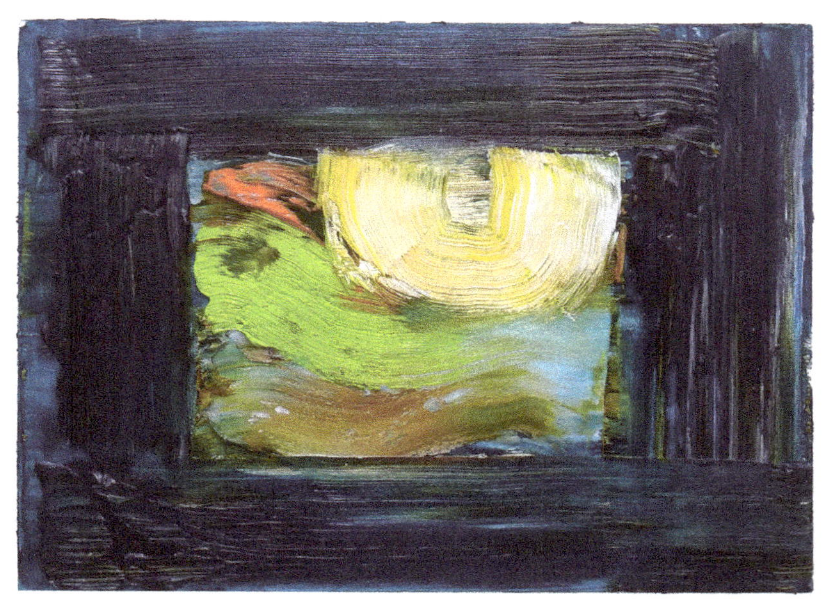

Robert Rhodes, *Quarantine: From the Garden Window*, 2020

Summer, Sheltering in Place

—after Robert Rhodes, *Quarantine: From the Garden Window*

When I was small, I used to wake before the sun
to sit in the still-dark living room, turn on the T.V.,
and bathe in the test pattern's bright glow. Now
that I so seldom leave the house, I lift the shade
at 5 AM, watch the colors rising one by one
outside the window, like an orchestra
in which one player at a time joins in until
a loud brightness stings my eyes, light
sifting through the leaves. Gradually,
that slash of green becomes the hedge,
the red smudge a neighbor's truck, backed
by a splash of blue, the pool across the street
the color of a cloudless sky. There's still an umber
patch of shadow underneath the trees.
In the branches of the sycamore, the woodpecker
listens hard, then mines the bark to find his breakfast.
Like me, grubs hidden there can't escape
his hammering. If I return this afternoon, the colors
will have dimmed or mellowed, the shadow disappeared.
What if the window's frame could suddenly
contain another scene, the veldt's burnt brown,
acacia like a stationary cloud, grazing zebras,
lions eying me through high grass? Remembering Monet,
I look and look again at the same view, find it changed
only by light, which after all, is everything.

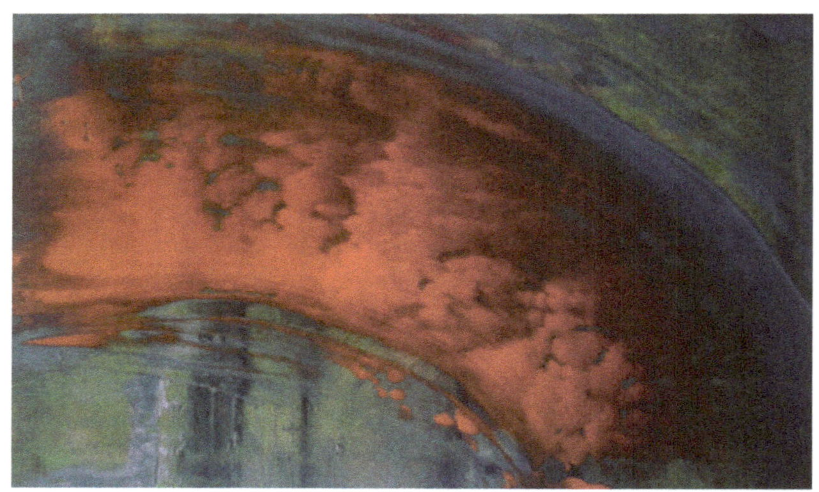

Robert Rhodes, *An Orange Gesture, A Memory of Light and Fire*

Night Painting

—after Robert Rhodes, *An Orange Gesture,*
   A Memory of Light and Fire

When at night I walk into the darkness under the tallest oaks
and see a burst of orange from the farthest stars,
the deepest past, rising high above the branches,
I know the light died out millions of years ago.
And yet, the stars burn holes into a green-gray cloud
that seems more sea than sky.
Everything yet to be born swims there.
Somewhere within the cloud,
past and present coexist.
Our galaxy, newly minted, not yet
faded to its milky hue, churns out the planets,
expanding like spheres of glowing glass,
blown hot from a handful of sand,
then plunged, hissing, into the icy sea.

Looking at Jupiter

In a kaleidoscope, shards of colored glass
drop into slots on a segmented wheel.
Red petals fall from a rose,
leaves from a tree,
then reattach.
When I turn to the window,
a red house appears, its pointed roof
tipped with flame.
A rainy afternoon offers umbrellas,
patterned like the underside of a frond
with unreadable braille.

We used to think space was empty,
full of dead rock, dark matter,
but here is Jupiter, tossing her orange scarves,
67 moons whirling around her
in orbits more intricate
than any Hollywood choreographer
could devise.
Ice matched with fire,
every hue that ever was.
Much depends on the flick of a wrist,
the position of the observer,
the play of light on clouds.

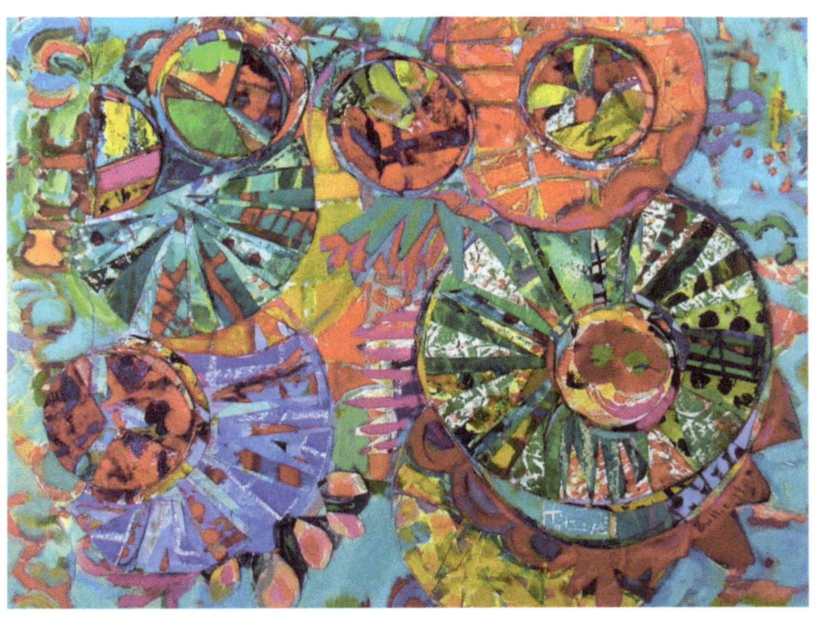

Mary Boxley Bullington, *Reinventing the Color Wheel*, 2010

Veils

—after Robert Rhodes, *Veils: A Room, a Door,*
a Light in the Upstairs Hall

Every evening, shadows lay their veils
over the familiar and the movie starts.
I pass my hand through the projector's dusty beam,
watch it weave a stream of motes into another world.
I hardly need to leave my room to see
the moon, perfectly composed
behind a screen of branches, transmute
the purple half-light from an open window,
playing for hours on the bedroom wall.

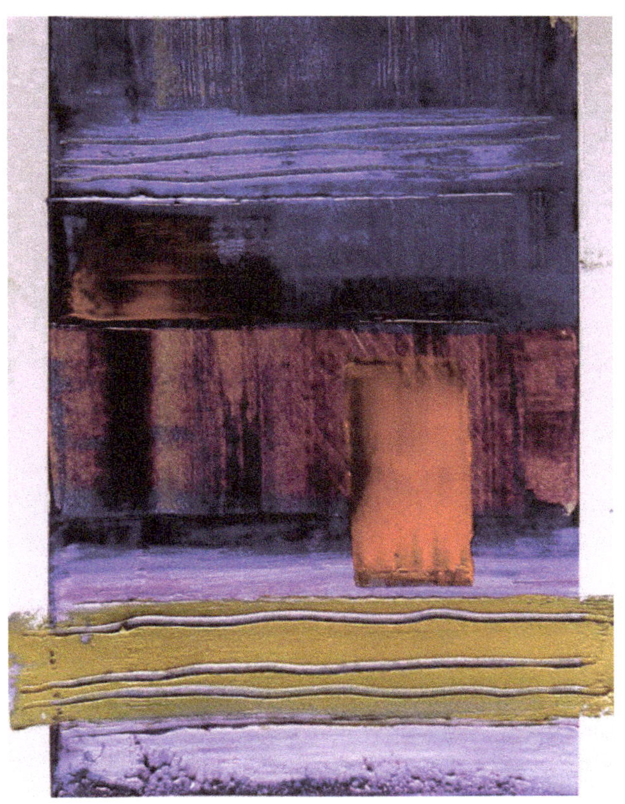

Robert Rhodes, *Veils: A Room, A Door, A Light in the Upstairs Hall*

Leonardo da Vinci, *A Copse of Trees,* 1508

Copse of Trees

For over five-hundred years, an island
of red birch trees has huddled in the top
right corner of a page, rootless in a field
of what might be snow, except for leaves
still covering the branches. It's a summer day
in scarlet, a negative un-developing in sunlight,
like the shadow-worlds I pondered
as a child, paging through my parents'
photo albums. But what if instead of
disappearing, like the sun behind the hill,
a snapshot of a life that used to be,
the drawing offers up its fragments
and loose ends, inviting us to weave
the fabric of a world that never was,
but could be, one we'd imagine
out of air if we commenced to dream?

Unspecified

—after Hans Arp, 1950s

This is the body as it was at the beginning—
neither male nor female, all soft folds.
A bulging bag full of eels,
it becomes as we watch
an elbow, a knee, a head
tilted upward, blank face
shining like the shadowed moon.

Momento Mütter

To wander these virtual halls, cabinet of human
anomalies, is to explore the body. Where else
would one find a grotesquely distended colon,
blasted as a blown fuse; wax cast of a syphilitic skull;
slices of Einstein's cerebellum sandwiched between
thin sheets of glass. In a glass case, centered
like a trophy, a plaster cast of the famous Chang
and Eng, the original Siamese twins, bound face
to face at the sternum by a thin band of skin,
hovers above the keyboard. One twin drank
heavily, while the other abstained. It must have
been awkward, living a joint life, even as the two
men married, conceived their own children, died.
How would it be to see your own face mirrored only
in the face of the other, to know what it meant
to be alone only when the other perished,
to carry that weight till it brought you down?

Pharmacy

—after Joseph Cornell, Pharmacy

Some say art has no purpose, yet
in this cabinet of curiosities, Cornell
puts this question to the test. Here,
he has collected pushpins and corks,
rubber bands and string, objects
any of us might assemble for later use.
But what of the cloud crammed into
a bottle, the cork pushed askew by its
insistent mass, wisp thin pencil shavings,
or dried fish, ready for a sauce or potion.
He has gathered the bright feathers
of tiny tropical birds, in case we might
wish, against the advice of the ancients,
to take flight, or to construct lures
for fly fishing, sharp-tipped arrows.
In one jar, the shells of sea snails
whisper to one another, curl like
commas. In another, gold paint
awaits a scribe to take up
the brush and ornament a page.

An Acorn, Beginning to Grow

—after a series of photographs by Beth Moon

This acorn is long, not squat, like those I played with as
    a child, making
caps for clothespin dolls. If no squirrel intrudes, no leaf
    blower or rake
sends it tumbling into the sewer, this acorn might
    eventually become
an oak. In these sequential shots, we see the first green
    corkscrew
spiral from the shell. It opens like a bud, each petal
    peeling from
the tight-shut core, as a mussel parts its lips to waves
    that bring it
nourishment. Rootlets begin to search the duff, making
    a space
to grow, to start the long unfolding that may go on for
    centuries.

Peasant Wedding

—after Bruegel, The Peasant Wedding

You can almost hear them,
busy at their feasting, can
almost smell the bread, the yeasty
brew. The bride sits in the center,
crowned with a chaplet, the only
still point in a scene so full
of movement. Eyes closed,
she dreams this day will
last forever. Her expression
echoes a Madonna's, but she's
dressed in green and black, not
transcendental blue. The palette's
mostly dark—black, brown, and
dun, a bit of green, except the servers'
crimson shirts and caps. This bride
is queen of Earth, not heaven.
Tomorrow she will labor at the
hearth and in the field. A shock
of wheat bisected by a scythe
reminds us that these revelers
hope for rain, not angels. The Lord
they know has claimed his place
at table, owns the land and all
that it produces. They trust
what grows, the certainty of
summer and the sun's warm grace.

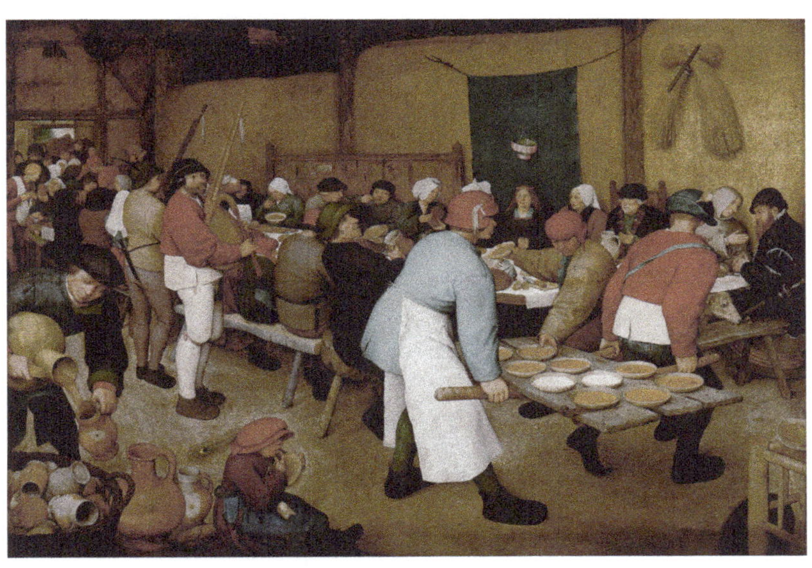

Pieter Brueghel the Elder, *The Peasant Wedding*, c. 1568

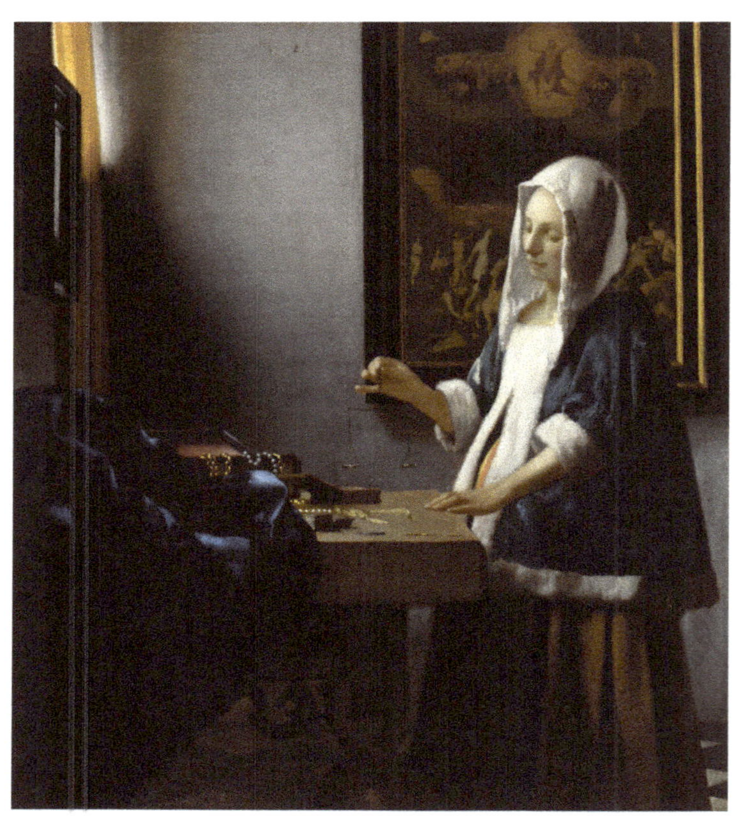

Johannes Vermeer, *Woman Holding a Balance*, 1664

In the Balance

—after Vermeer, *Woman Holding a Balance*

She's an earthly icon, serene in blue and white,
eyes lowered to the golden scale as though
at prayer. Yet she's dressed in rich brocade,
sleeves trimmed with ermine. Pearls and gold
glow before her, like the moon through
tangled branches. Behind her, an image
of the Last Judgment, where souls are weighed
and measured, fitted for heaven or its alternative.
For Vermeer, the light and shadows, tones
and folds of fabric, the body and its rucks and pleats,
are next to heaven, though they do not last.
Without them, there would be no art, no heaven
we could imagine. The spirit on one side
of the balance; on the other, the scents,
the substance, and the color of this world.

Adaptation

On Adaptation

—inspired by Arkhip Kuindzhi, *After a Rain;*
Andrei Tarkovsky, *Solaris;* and *Solaris,*
a novel by Stanislaw Lem

I peer from the portal, afraid to find
some portion of my past projected
on the mirror surface of this alien
world. The field beside the barn
takes shape as I watch, wrenched
whole from its foundation in memory,
dropped like a seed onto what had been
bare rock between two continents.
In this incarnation, the rain has just
ended, will soon begin again.
Dark clouds brood over the fields,
flashing, phosphorescent,
like deep-sea jellyfish. I suppose
at home we'd call this night,
and yet it isn't quite, something other
than the ordinary. Cows still browse,
yet the sky, spent by the storm,
has at last left off illuminating
the surface of the planet,
a task taken up by this bright meadow,
this farm, simulacrum of our green island, Earth.

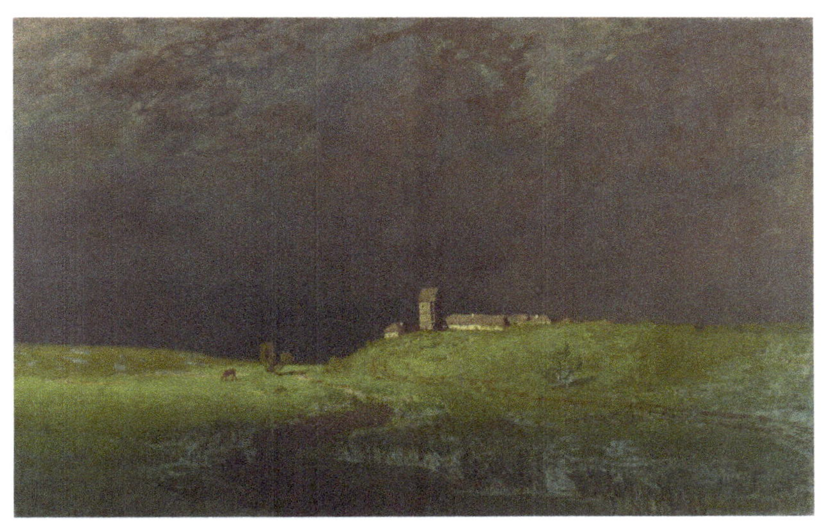

Arkhip Kuindzhi, *After a Rain*, 1879

Her Complaint

—after Andrea Kowch, *In the Distance*

Something's always rising, whether sun or wind or sudden
flames flaring in the old oak after a storm. Just now, more
loaves are proofing in the oven, dough unfolding, doubling.
So many mouths, all of them hungry. The world's voracious,
and I must feed these hungers with these hands, this body,
kneading, rolling out the dough. Even at night, after the baking's
done, no rest. I am kneaded in my turn, the soft mounds
of my breasts, my belly, always making something new
out of the substance I've been given, rising to the task.

Dangerous Dreams

—after Thomas Terceira, *Metamorphosis 1*

A man who envies all creatures avian, even
the flightless kind, with stumpy, rudimentary
flippers where their wings would be,
wakes one morning with a black arc of feathers
welded to his spine, less a bird's wing
than a dinosaur's dorsal ridge.
He dreams of flight, but with this
clumsy appendage will never take to air—
not without the aid of ordinary
human transportation. The single wing
makes shopping for a shirt embarrassing.
If only he could emulate the flying squirrel,
with its appealing fur and webbed appendages,
so much easier to hide beneath a suitcoat.
Before the change, he'd always been
a man, inside the Alcatraz of human form,
affecting a feathery goatee, an affinity for high branches.

American Gothic

—after Grant Wood, *American Gothic*

Weathered as the barn behind them,
hard-eyed and narrow, this pair
has a history that never needs to be spoken—
all the bad harvests, floods, ill fortune.
A few sparks shielded between their palms.
What little they own they built themselves.
No patience for roses. When they look
at the golden fields, they see only
what those sheaves will buy—a new roof,
some boots, a mule. They teach this
bitter wisdom: we must wrestle
this angel, the earth, until it yields,
must take what we can
before the storm comes,
before we return to dust.

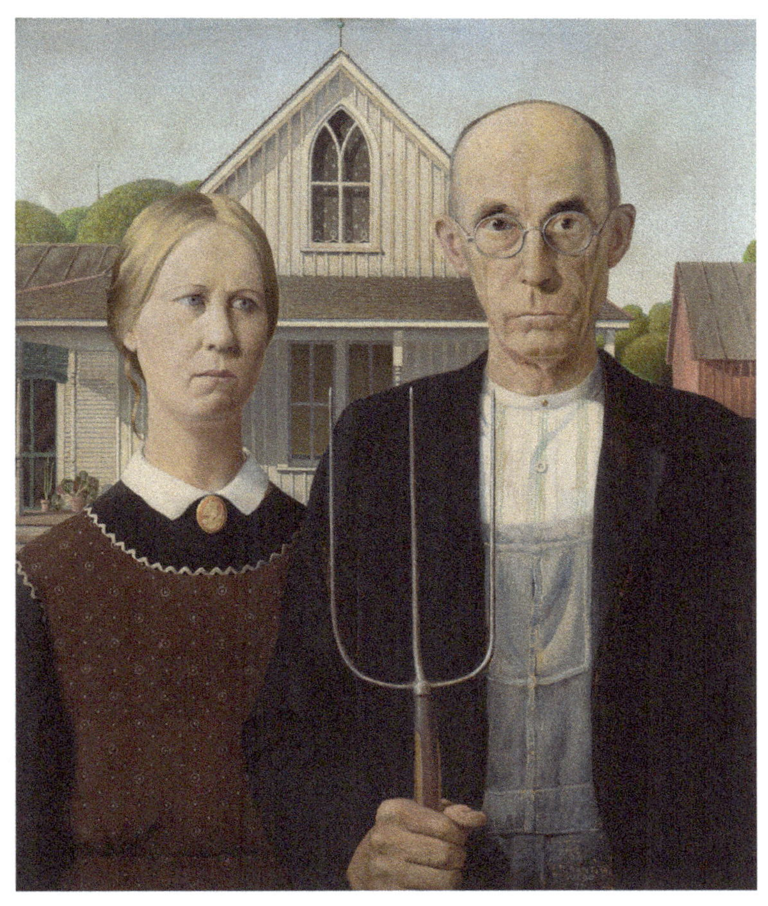

Grant Wood, *American Gothic*, 1930

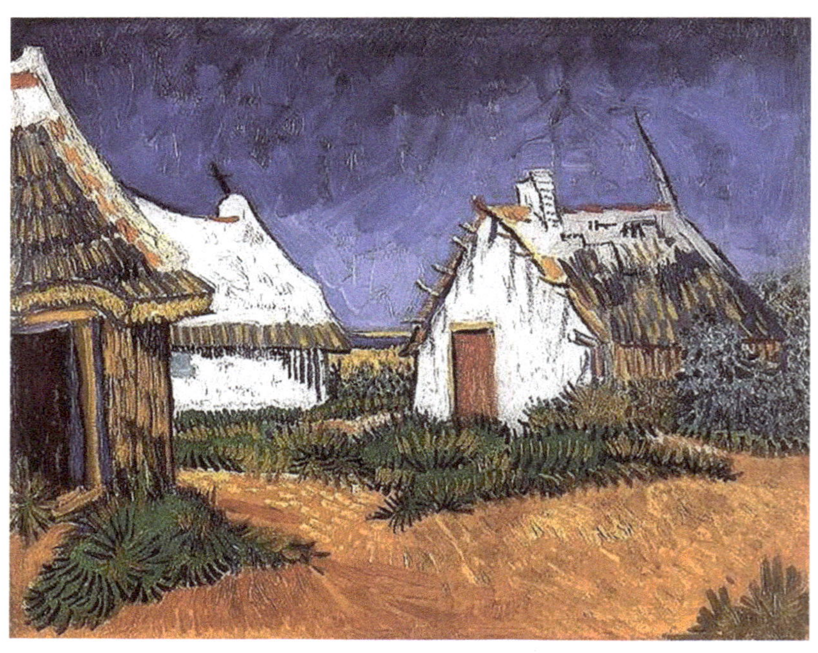

Vincent van Gogh, *Three White Cottages in Saintes-Maries*, 1888

Three White Cottage

As native to this landscape
as the spiky grass, these cottages
are like the stunted forest I once saw
half-buried in the dunes, branches
still blossoming. They persist,
facing away from the ocean,
as though denying it, as does
the village, rooted on a berm.
The church, conspicuous against
a sea-blue sky, is less a rock
than hayrick, cross tilting on a roof
of whitewashed thatch. One good
storm could bring it down.
The other cottage sports a spar,
a splinter rising from the roof,
mast without a jib. The third
is less a cottage than a swell
of straw, offering a view
of sea grass swaying
in a breeze. Together,
these houses have mastered
the art of being tenuous.
Bright as a box of crayons,
the sky and land vibrate
with light. Is it evening
or full day? The houses sail
each night through a sky
of phosphorescent sparks, nary
a husk of moon to mark the way.

Winter

> —after Robert Rhodes, *Winter: Farm Road, Lancaster County*

Twenty-seven seeds sleep in the frozen ground,
the grass shielding them shorn to yellow stubble.
From the pane, the fields seem sere and still,
but I remind myself of what I cannot see:
If I took a spade this moment to the cold earth,
steam would rise from the depths where roots
and tubers chart their path through darkness,
and everything waits to emerge into the warm light.

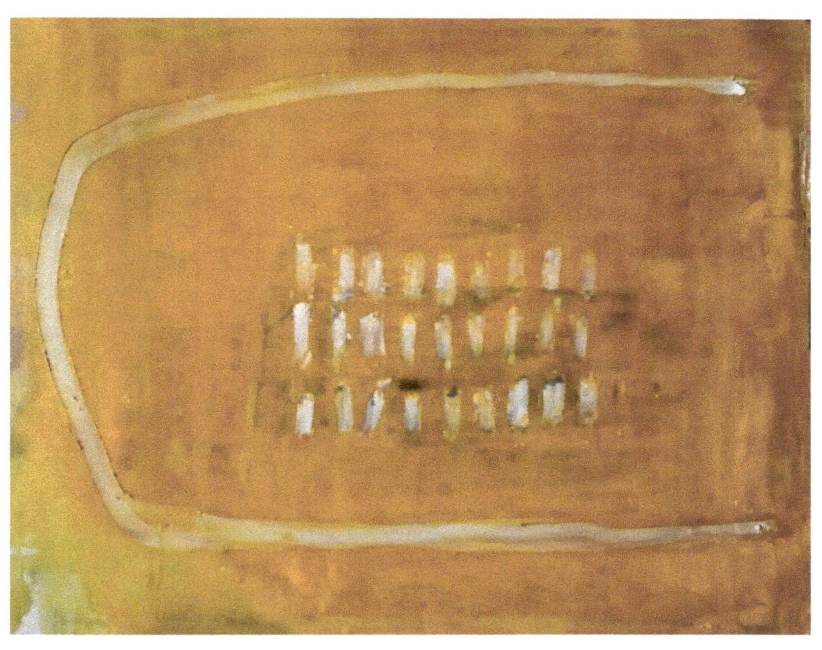

Robert Rhodes, *Winter: Farm Road, Lancaster County*, 2020

Evolving Sirenian

Everything in the ocean
becomes something else.
Colonies of coral, once
a soft carpet of color,
become brittle and white,
the stuff of island sand.
The octopus embodies
this quality of change.
Exactly the shape of whatever
it needs to be, the octopus pours
itself between two rocks.
In the painting, its tentacles curl
like breakers, tangled kelp fronds.

Caught in the act of transformation,
the octopus takes on
the blue and orange
of a large carcass, flesh peeling
in flakes from its side.
Then it disappears, skin
puckering in mock putrescence,
eye gaping like a wound.

No wonder sailors wandering
at sea once mistook this creature
for a woman, hair trailing behind her
in the green-blue surf,
singing the most beautiful song.

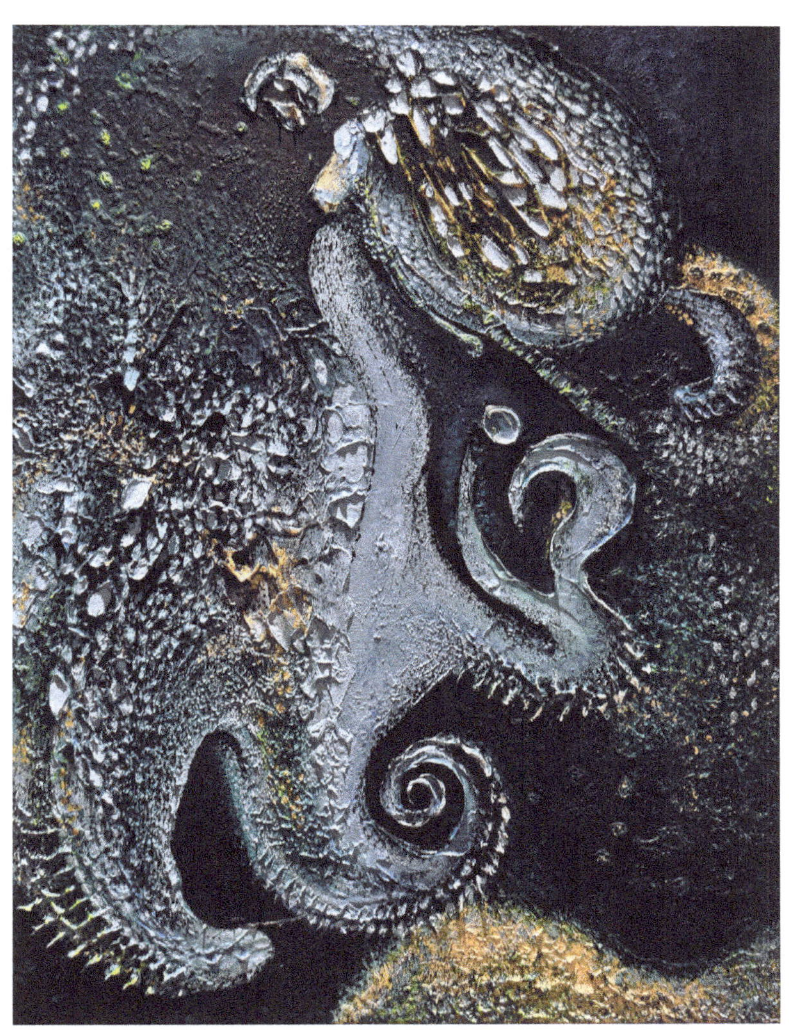

Sallie Swift, *Evolving Sirenian*, 2012

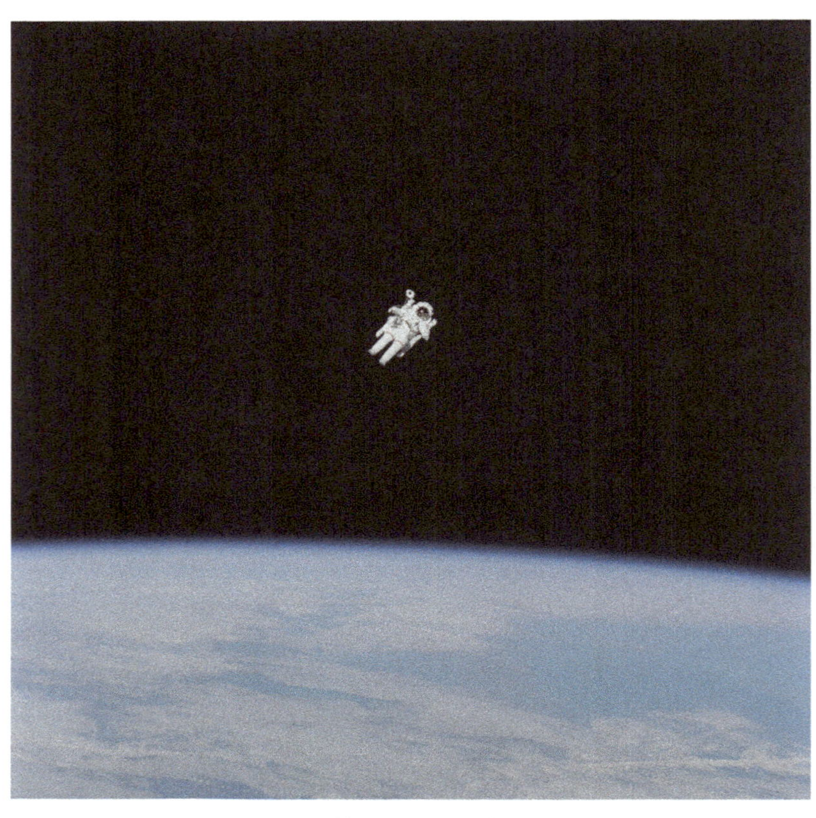

Bruce McCandless II, on February 7, 1984,
became the first person to make an untethered spacewalk.

Two Ways of Taking Up Space

—after a NASA photograph

1

Faceless in his pressure suit
and helmet, he hangs perpetually
between, privileged to witness
our planet from outside the barrier
of cloud that keeps us
from knowing where we stand.
So small against the dark
immensity—the planet
and its minuscule inhabitant,
first man to see
how vulnerable we are.

2

Closer to home, more metaphorical,
the perfect embodiment of trauma--
the way she feels whenever
the cold mood takes her:
unmoored above the bright
world that goes on—as it
always has--without her.

Fitting

—after Rupert Jessup

I. The Tailor

He fashions suits and dresses
out of silk and scraps—the point's
the process, tiny identical
stitches orbiting the buttonholes,
hems and cuffs turned like
hospital corners, the fabric's
immaculate fit. He must
make each piece to order
for its own sake, transform
the ordinary. After measuring
the body, he'd rather not
look back at it again, preferring
to imagine the ideal. This red
gown will hang like a Chinese
Maple leaf ready to fall, the body
a whisper under the weave.
From the bodice, with its tiny
tucks and folds, will rise
the shoulders, the head on its
stem of neck, the upswept
nape-- a violet, just
burst from the bud.

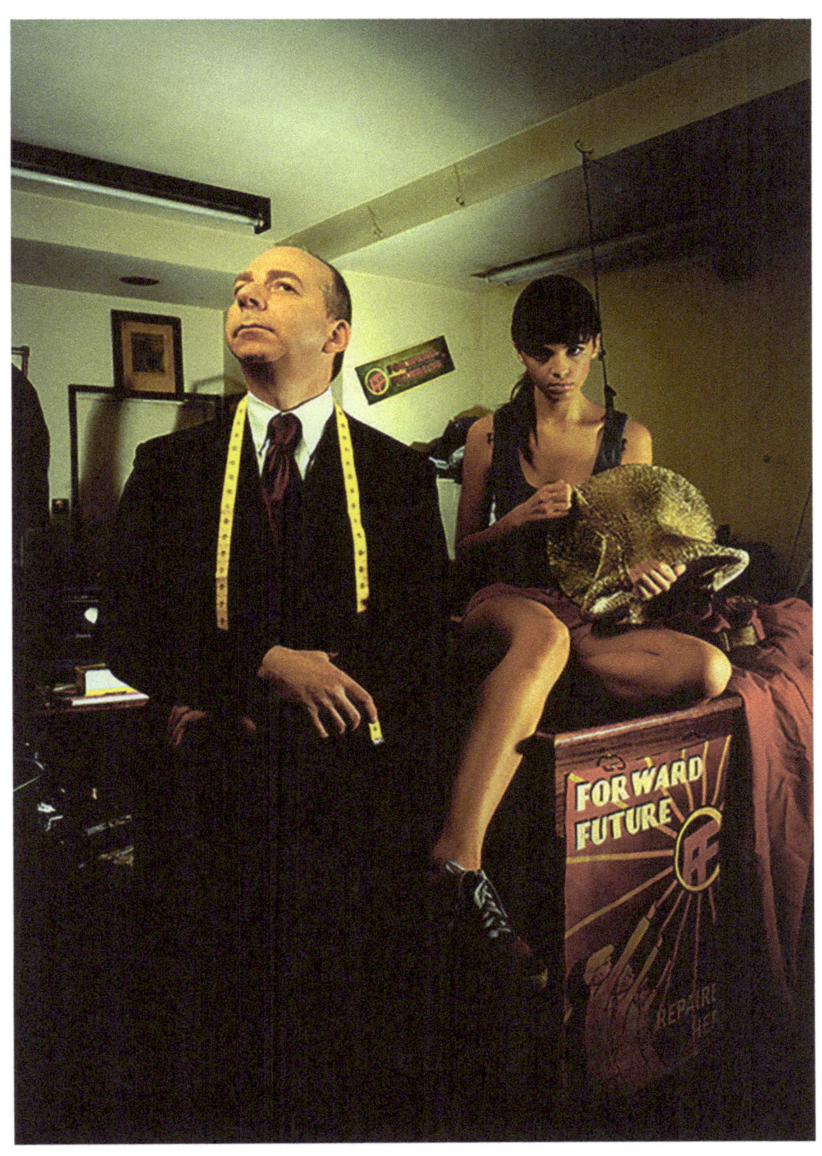

Rupert Jessup, *Fitting*

II. The Girl

I ought to be wearing
nothing but my own
smooth skin. To please
others, I bind my body
in silk, a pale lacewing fly
caught in a web of social
conventions. They have
decreed I must teeter
on tight, pointed shoes.
The tailor, consulting his
measurements, never looks
into my eyes, hardly sees me.
In this he is no different
from so many others, with their
ready-made notions of who
I am, who I ought to be.

Once a Raven

—after Beth Moon, *Flight of the Raven*

In another life, we flew together,
sheltered in the boughs
of ancient bristlecones, rich with seed.
Our voices rose, loud and raucous.
But that was long ago, almost
beyond memory. From the ground,
I watch the flocks assemble on the wires,
the stunted eucalyptus. They call to one another
in a tongue I no longer understand.

Seeker of bright things, there is only
one way back to harmony.
With you at my back, like a quiver,
I become a corvid angel, hunting nothing
but the sense of flight,
intimate with clouds and wind.
My human bones are clumsy,
far too heavy for this feat, yet I rise
unencumbered on borrowed wings,
adept in ways forgotten long ago.

Disquiet

—after Kylli Sparre, *Disquiet*

On the ocean floor, sleeping groupers camouflage
themselves as rocks, cocoon in clouds of sand
and mucus spun out of the substance of their
bodies, as spiders' spinnerets let down a line
of silk. I'm like that, like the whelk within
its fortress of a shell, shielded in a vaporous
swirl. It doubles as a dress of white
chiffon, inverted parachute that spirals
around my body like vanilla soft serve,
ribbon of cream in coffee. When I feel
threatened, the dress sets up its own
internal wind and weather, swallows me
whole. At the first sign of threat, it
automatically inflates. I take flight
on milky tides of moonbeams,
streamers of phantom light.

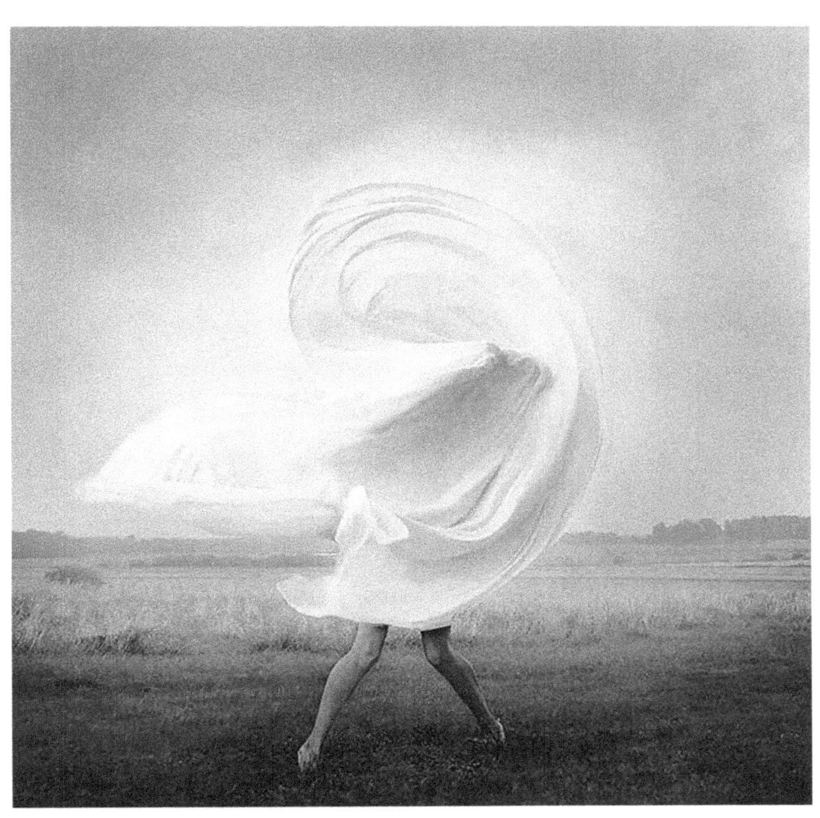

Kylli Sparre, *Disquiet*, 2019

The Harem Speaks

He imagines that his clothing,
thick with embroidery,
effort of our invisible sisters,
the royal seamstresses,
invests him with power,
but we know that underneath
all the work of our hands,
he is scarcely more substantial than smoke,
his withered white thighs,
and the limp herring
resting between them.
The crown tips sideways on his disorderly hair
like an abandoned crow's nest.

In contrast, we stand
naked before him,
one of us almost featureless.
The other holding her face before her,
a mask she cannot drop.
We share a cloud of hair.
But this as well is an illusion.
Inside us swells the seed of power.
We wax as he wanes,
his belly great only
with foul air.
Now it is the artist's brush,
his pencil, that rises.
The king is done with such acts.
He can only gaze at our firm flesh,
our splendor.
We bide our time.

Sea Star

We have heard of selkies and mermaids,
women who shed the burden of their human
skin and take the form of sea creatures, seals
or hybrid beasts. But no fabulist I know of
has yet imagined that a woman might embrace
a sea star's form. Invertebrate, radially symmetrical,
moving so oddly on its myriad feet it seems
a composite rather than a single beast, this
creature has an eye on every arm. It has
the power to regenerate its parts, and sometimes,
cut in half, has been known to mend its body
if the vital organs have been spared.
Anyone might envy this power. So perhaps
it's not surprising that the woman in the deck
chair, weary of her life on this side of the ocean,
might desire a sea star's life, so she gradually
assumes this form, lengthening first one leg,
then another. Her hair retreats into her scalp,
the neck and head preparing to become
yet another arm. In one last action of her
human mind, she sends a message in a bottle
into the surf, telling her story to the waiting world.

The Transformation

—after Aggie Zed, *Magician*

Enchantment overtakes us from within.
What we become amounts to what we are.
The magician's gift is cruel that way:
it gives him pleasure to expose
the secret self. Here, it's a snake that struggles
to emerge, like toothpaste, out of the victim's
human pores. His stunned hands
shape the air, his voice the soft hiss
of a punctured tire escaping from
what used to be his mouth, slipped
sideways like a scythe, his head
now covered by a burlap sack, the kind
once used to blindfold the condemned.
And yet we guess that really, under
the sack, he has no face at all, no split
tongue testing the air, only an expression
of the flux itself. And now the anaconda
coils enfold his torso, consume his hybrid body.

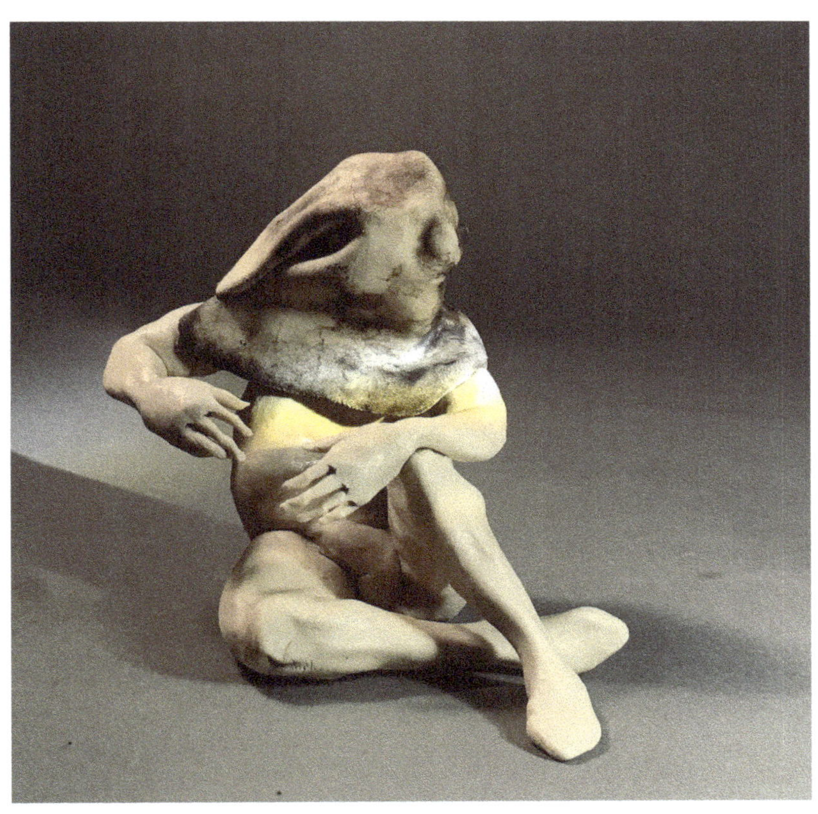

Aggie Zed, *Magician*, 2001

Flamingo in Lake Natron, Northern Tanzania

—after Nick Brandt, *Petrified Flamingo, Lake Natron*

From above, the lake seems a kind of paradise,
the breeding ground of many migratory birds.
Already, flocks dot the shore. Yet the water teems
with hundreds of fallen birds looking for a place
to stretch and preen.

Those lured by the mirror of the lake's red water,
so bright it's visible from space, will die in this
runoff from the volcano, Ol Doinyo Lengai.
Their feathers harden into clumps of brittle string,
flattened winter weeds. Their wings lie heavy,
will never feel the touch of air again.

The hollow reeds that were their legs stuck fast
in silt, the boiling water thick as blood,
a bitter brew has turned them all to salt.

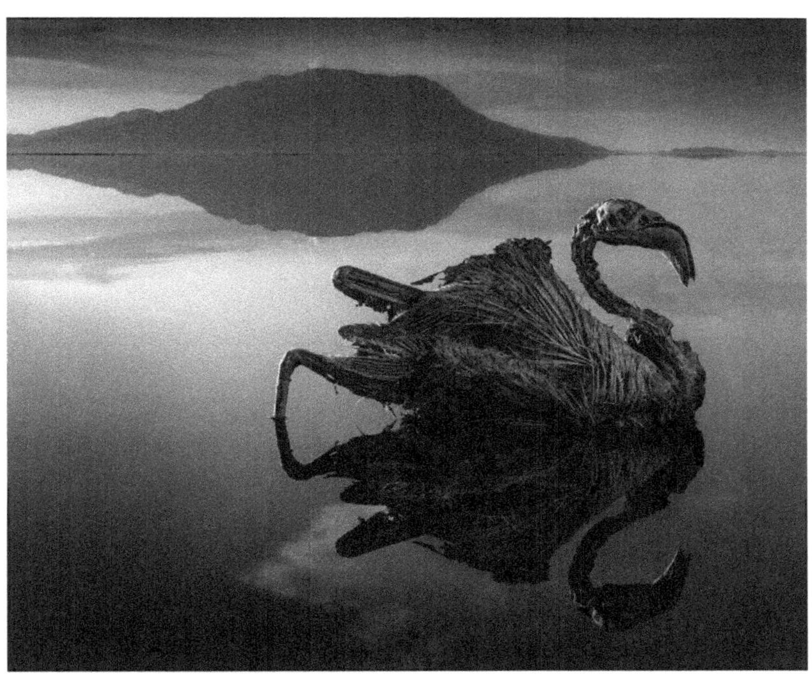

Nick Brandt, *Petrified Flamingo, Lake Natron*, 2013

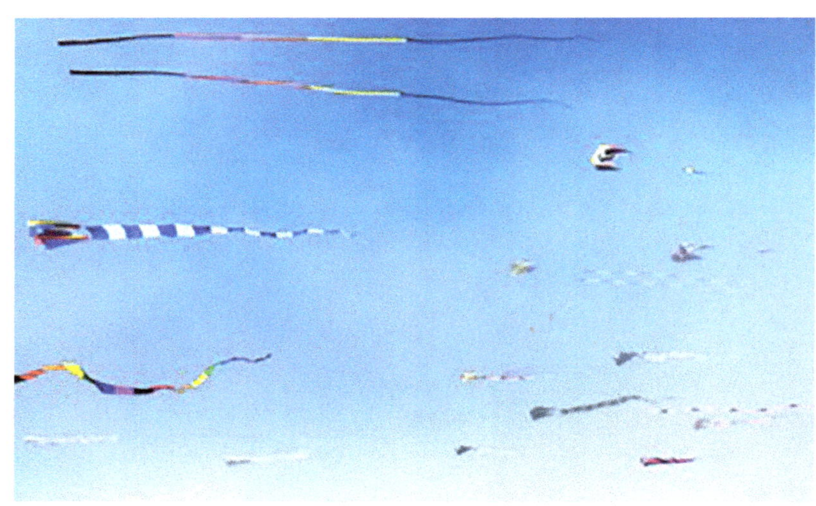

Sally Gall, *Heavenly Creatures #2*

Love Letter to the Sky

—after Sally Gall, Heavenly Creatures

The sky's a bolt of azure silk
stretched tight as I ascend,
trailing a Man O' War tail
behind me. My body bells
with the breeze. Among
the others, content to dip
and soar like butterflies,
plankton beneath a lens,
only I desire to keep on
going, beyond the border
where the blue shades
into blackness, and the stars
blink on. Only I will dare
to voyage, then return,
bright body intact. It's just
a thread that holds me, taut
string that might at any minute
snag or snap. The wind
might flag and send me
tumbling. Given a chance,
If I were lifted by a sudden
gust too powerful for string
and paper, would I wish to rise
and rise, never look back?

Law of Attraction

Law of Attraction

—after Vincent van Gogh,
    Starry Night Over the Rhone

The world's a watery reflection—
only the sky seems solid, thick
with stars, vibrating like struck bells.
Golden ripples of light radiate
into the river, stars diving
below the surface
in showers of sparks and steam.
In its turn, the river rises out of its basin,
sleepwalking toward the surf.
The sea, reaching for the shore,
takes a bit of land each time
it sweeps the sand. Even proud
mountains give themselves to waves
and wind, wear down to a pebble,
and are borne away.

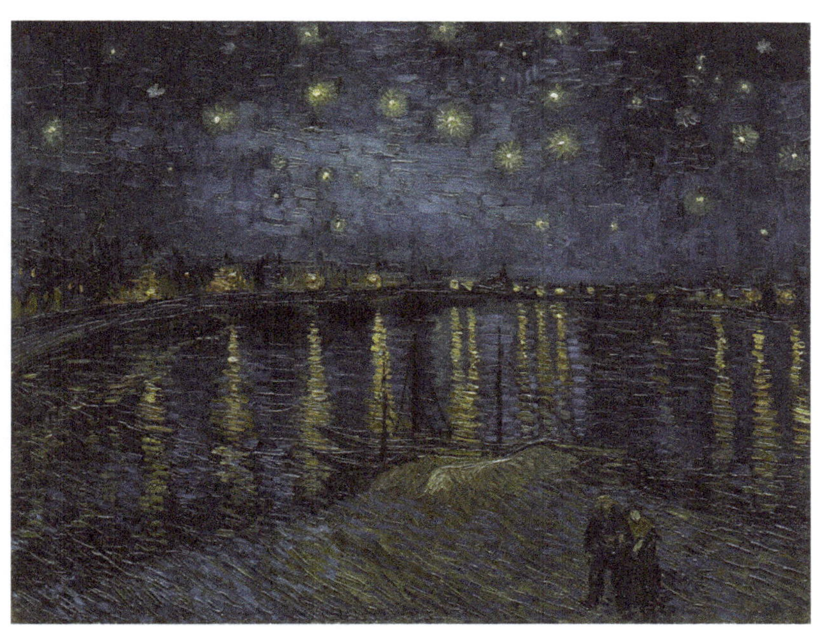

Vincent van Gogh, *Starry Night Over the Rhone*, 1888

The Lives of a River

—after Magan Ruthke, *Wisdom in the Missouri*

The Mississippi and Amazon, the brown Missouri
and Orinoco, the Susquehanna.
Whether sullied by smokestacks and fertilizer,
reflecting the tallest buildings or the largest
trees, frequented by long-legged herons
or roseate spoonbills, by toxic waste
or spring meadows, each travels its own path,
carves through mountains or crosses deserts,
percolates down to limestone caverns, to the
most hidden of aquifers, here narrowing
to almost nothing, there swelling to a loud torrent,
through branches and tributaries,
confluence or delta, till it reaches the sea.
Then it surrenders, becomes a single part
of something much larger. But for a while,
the river remains itself, sometimes recognizable
in a tint or a shade, a sound, a peculiar counter-current
underlying the ocean's larger surge, a chorus
of hundreds of voices speaking at once.
For that small time, the river remains
as particular as the pattern of hand-woven cloth,
or the split skin of the anaconda, still bearing
the snake's sightless sockets, draped whole
from a branch or fallen in shreds to the ground,
the muscle gone out of it. We can still trace
the corners of the flexible jaws, capable of taking in
prey bigger around than the snake itself.
The sea too is like this, accepting,
the place where all of us begin and end.

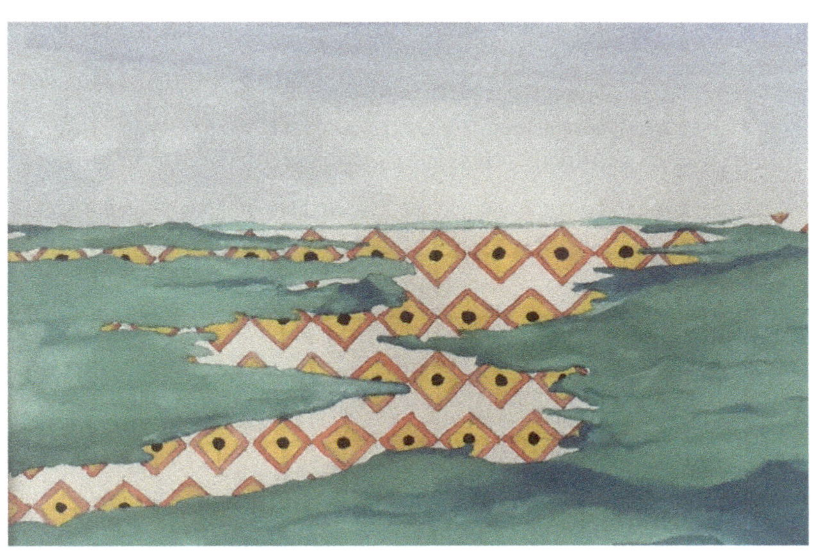

Magan Ruthke, *Wisdom in the Missouri*, 2017

Avenue of Oaks

—after Beth Moon, *Avenue of Oaks*, 2006

The Earth's forgotten when
someone planted acorns here
in two straight lines, anticipating shade,
a bed of soft black soil beneath the leaves
where travelers could rest, refuge
for nesting larks and falcons
scanning the winter skies for prey.

In summer, overhanging leaves
and branches form a canopy.
The trunks still stand alone,
two separate lines of trees
just as they always were.
But below, their white roots mingle,
less a group than one expression
of the urge to grow, a single being.

Gogol's Dream

—after Victor Gontarov, *Gogol's Dream*, 1995

In the world of dream and nightmare, not
found on any map, dark houses conspire,
leaning toward each other like volumes
on an overcrowded shelf, titles effaced,
pages foxed and folded, swollen with rain.
In this shadow of his native Poltava, his books
haunt the frozen fields. Derelict windmills
gesture in a weak breeze. A pine sapling
takes improbable root in the rock-hard river,
where just lately, a startled fisherman
expecting a net full of gravid sturgeon
hauled out instead a piscine Madonna,
adrift on an oval of ice, a woman, gripped
to the pubis by a large-mouthed pike. It is she
whom he worships, holding out his heart
like an automaton, a bright bouquet,
as, clutching her own white waterlily,
she looks away.

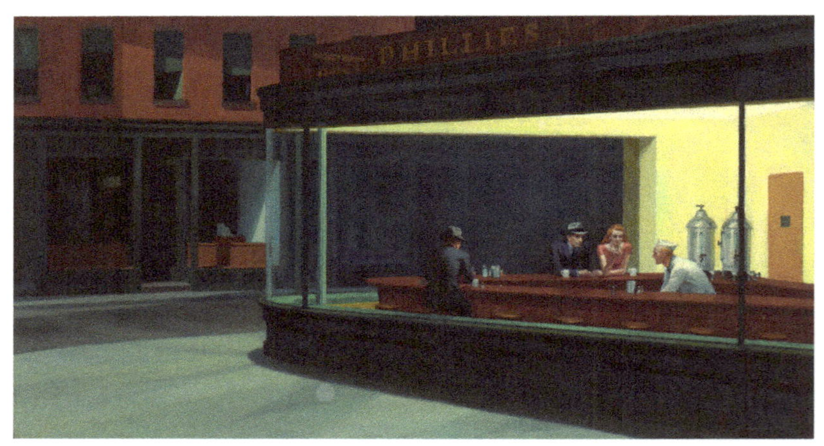

Edward Hopper, *Nighthawks*, 1942

Nighthawks

—after Edward Hopper, *Nighthawks*

We're voyeurs, watching from a distance,
absently observing the street. And how
could we avoid it? The storefront glows
like an aquarium, inviting inspection,
its art deco exterior curved, sleek as a shark,
a Bentley cruising the block. The four
specimens behind the glass might have
emerged from a dream or diorama, a Disney
vision of the future, all gleaming surfaces,
already obsolete--the men in their hats
and suits, the woman in her red dress,
the silver urns of coffee dispensing wakefulness.
Believing that seeing implies understanding,
we study the two men seated at the counter,
those doppelgangers. The one at the far left
corner observes the couple (if that's what they are),
sitting silent before their coffee. It's a closed system;
no way in or out, suggesting that even things seen
most clearly remain essentially unknown, unknowable.

Girl Interrupted

—after Vermeer, *Girl Interrupted at her Music*

No music here, just sheets
of silent notes, excuse
for furtive glances,
momentary touch,
foray of fingers on the field of song.
A glass of wine waits on the table,
garnet bright, as though just poured.
The artist, with his eye for nuance,
gift for light, has intruded
on this private scene that might,
without our probing glances,
develop into something more.
It's all about a moment of potential.

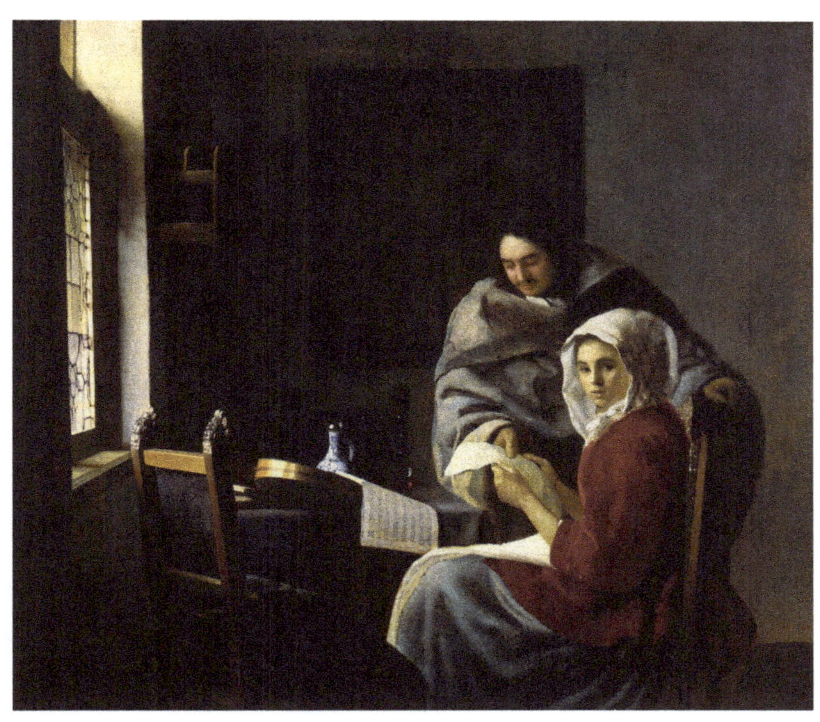

Johannes Vermeer, *Girl Interrupted at Her Music*, c. 1658–61.

El Jaleo

—after John Singer Sargent, *El Jaleo*

I've been to this party, where the men
stroke the strings of sad guitars,
hiding their faces beneath broad-brimmed
hats, melancholy and preoccupied,

while on the other side of the room,
the women sway in their seats,
drawn by the dance, the dancer.
Their faces shimmer in the half-light,
a field of poppies, and the dancer,
goddess in white, frothy black mantilla
draped over her shoulders, turns toward
the eager women, tosses them a rose.

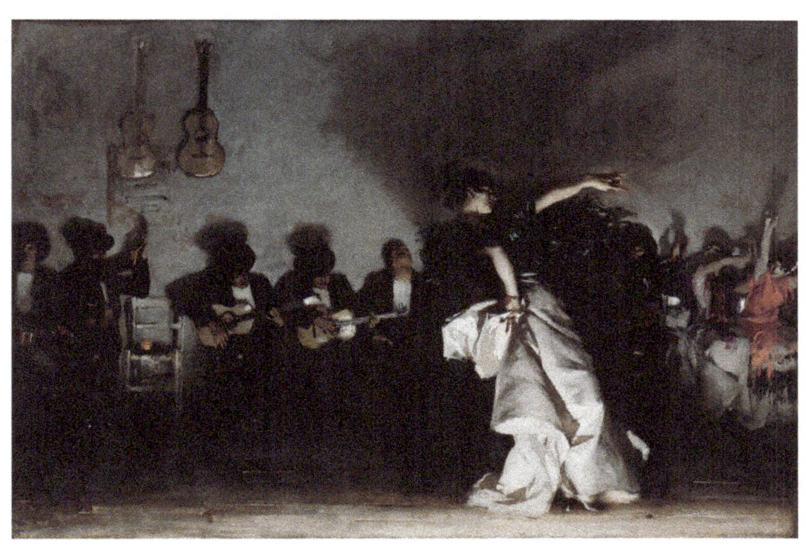

John Singer Sargent, *El Jaleo*, 1882

Fog and Moonlight

—after Robert Rhodes, *Fog and Moonlight:*
Margaret in her Nightgown, Alone in Bella's Yard

Mist rose from the grass into a sky
just beginning to grow light.
You threw off the rumpled sheets,
glided down the stairs and out the door,
leaving it open behind you, seeing
the yard transformed, the pedestrian
birdbath, close-cropped grass
masked by fog. Posing like a dancer,
you turned your face up to the moon,
as though it were a mirror
and you an ingenue, as though you knew
that I was watching from behind the open door.
And then, wishes spent, you stretched
under the oak, white shreds of fog
caught in your hair, and slept.

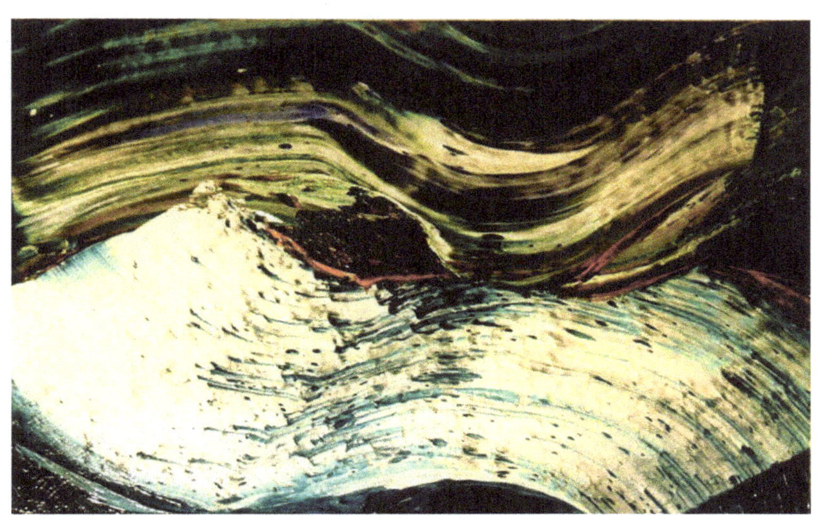

Robert Rhodes, *Fog and Moonlight:*
Margaret in her Nightgown, Alone in Bella's Yard, 2023

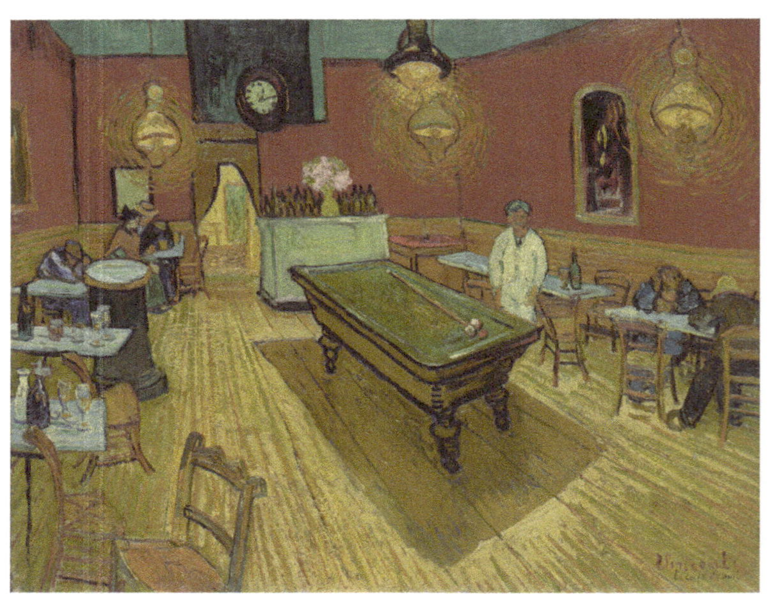

Vincent van Gogh, *The Night Café*, 1888.

Holy Hive

—inspired by Vincent van Gogh,
The Night Café

It's late, but the café glows:
its firefly fixtures, bright orange
walls like the inside of a tulip,
and I, a bee, come lately
from the fields, entering
the enclosed chamber, hushed
as a chapel. Intent on my dizzy flight,
I hardly see the others at their tables,
as in monastic cells, bowed low
over their glasses. Light as breath,
acolyte of sweetness, I approach
the altar of the pool table,
where ivory balls cricket-click,
create such harmony
I feel blessed just to be here,
to spend a quiet evening
with my own kind.

Still Standing

—after David Graeme Baker, *Ivy and Winslow*

At first glance, I think she is a teacher
drawing on the chalkboard. One finger
rests on the crevice where the chalk is kept.
The other arm sweeps wide, into an arc
on the board's murky green surface,
where transparent moon-jellies swarm:
words poorly erased. She drafts a magic
circle to protect her. Yet her feet are bare,
standing in a pool of long-dried paint,
as in a spotlight. I decide this is an abandoned
school, site of a shooting, now her studio,
where she can drop the line of her imagination,
netting the unexpected, lost voices of a thousand
children and their teachers. She probes a past
she doesn't really know, like a scientist who
studies creatures making their own cold light
in the deepest ocean, dreams and dreams again
about this ruined room, its light and shadows,
settled dust, compelled to paint it in bright hues,
to return and make this place a kind of shrine,
left standing to remind us of all that has been lost.

Ad Nihilum

Woman with Iguanas

—after Holly Wilmuth, *The Iguana
or Benevolent Dragon*

Perhaps there are crickets in her hair,
this woman wearing a hood of lizards,
face framed by their clawed toes,
tails crossed beneath her chin
like the roots of orchids. The lizards
clamber up her shoulders, grasp
her hair as though it were their customary
vines, the luckiest or the quickest
perching on her crown like trapeze
artists balanced on a narrow ledge.
She's a jungle, every inch alive.
Rain fills and overflows the bromeliads'
many goblets, crowned with extravagant
pink blooms. Aside from these, this world's
the unrelenting green of walking palm,
pot-bellied Barriconda. The woman endures,
because she must: she knows explorers
will eventually arrive to cut down trees and turn
them into cash, to capture wide-winged
Morphos, loud hyacinth macaws, to plunder
all her riches and leave her bare and brown.

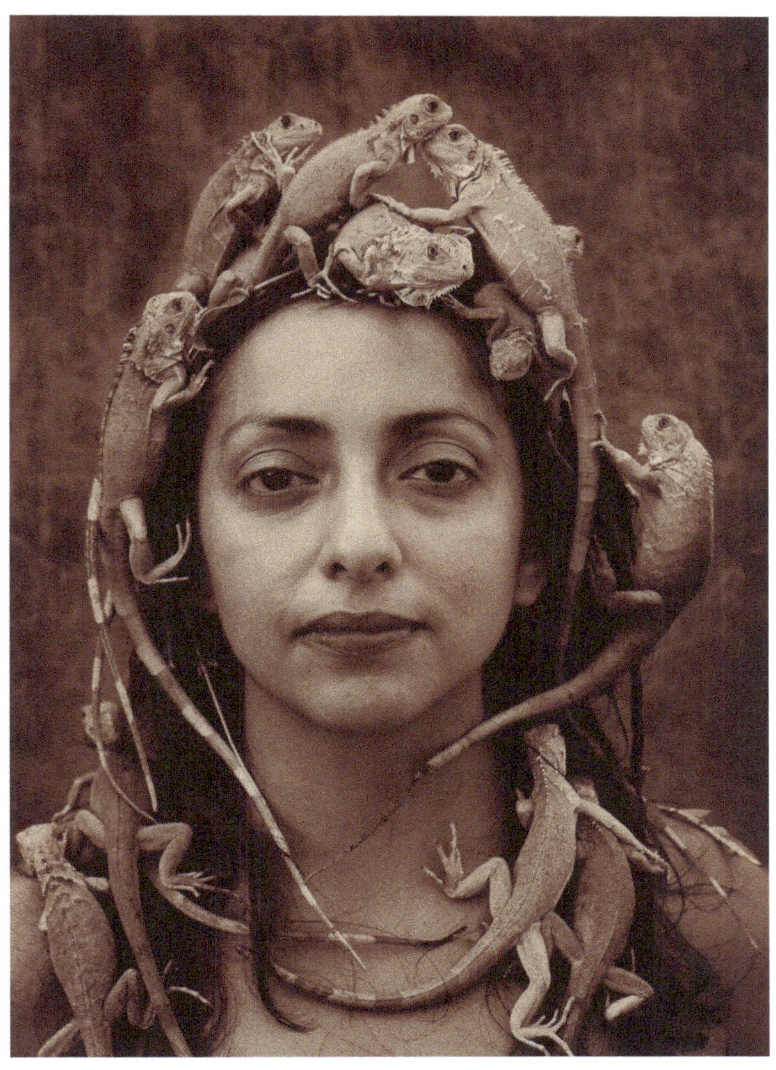

Holly Wilmuth, *The Iguana or Benevolent Dragon*, 2014

The Cloud Plague

—after Doc Blanchard, *Out by Dave's Place*

Out by Dave's place, the clouds touched the earth,
swallowing the cows and fields. Trees still bloom,
as always, covered with soap-bubble blossoms,
bursting from the naked branches after rain,
but when the petals fall, you can't see those
branches for all that whiteness. Nobody dares
step out into the field to probe with a toe
for the vanished ground. At first, we just
threw stones, listened for the sound
they'd make, hitting rocks and trees,
but hearing nothing, fled, afraid
that we'd be swallowed up as well.
Scientists arrived from the university,
skirting the edges of the meadow,
taking notes. They've built fences,
hoping to contain the clouds, but you
can't really hold a cloud or keep it in place.
We hope the land and everything we've lost
will someday reappear, the rocks and bushes,
the patchy grass, with its resident gophers
and squirrels, crabgrass, those things
we always thought would outlast us.

October is Burning

—after Robb Shaffer, *Biltmore Backyard*

In autumn, standing among
the trees, dressed perpetually
in their finery, I hunger for seasons,
the small fires of October
burning fields to the root,
skies suffused with smoke,
reducing summer to ash, to
leaf mold and yellow sheaves,
a ribbon of migrating geese
overhead, each bird sounding
its convivial trumpet.
Naked oaks, late-season
bathers caught in a chill,
spread their silver branches,
catching a last bit of sun.
Covens of pines summon
winter; the smallest Japanese
maples burst into flame.

The Burning

—after J. M. W. Turner, *The Burning
of the Houses of Lords and Commons,
16 October 1934*

At first it was simply the buildings,
an evening fit for a postcard,
triumphant avenues, gas lamps
rivaling the stars. But on the day
appointed to apply the final
coat of varnish, Turner instead,
before an audience of onlookers,
set the buildings blazing.
As they watched, fire flowed
in red and yellow strokes
across the water, unmaking
all it touched. With a twist
of brush, the witnesses appeared,
watching from small boats
and the opposing shores.
In the gallery, onlookers observed
as it took shape, a pattern
of un-being, picture of flux.

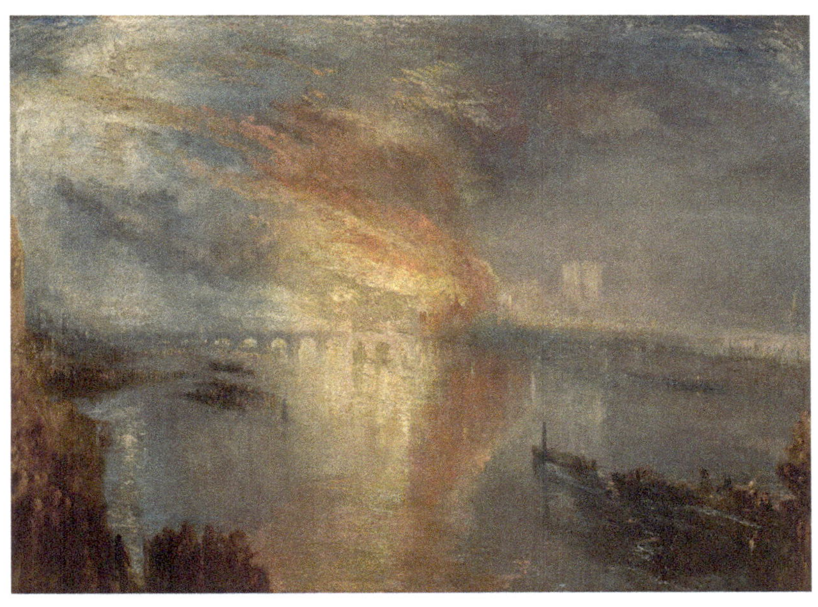

J. M. W. Turner, *The Burning of the Houses of Lords and Commons,*
16 October 1934, 1834

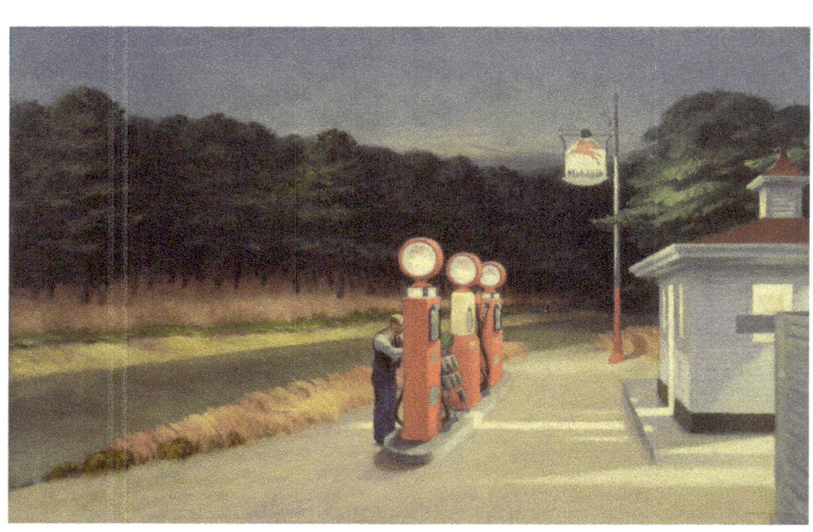

Edward Hopper, *Gas*, 1940

Shrine

—after Edward Hopper, *Gas*

Three totems stand in a pool of light,
just off the empty highway.
Each pump stares at the dark road,
howls with its o of a mouth at the rising
moon. A man without a car stands
beside the pump, head bent, properly
reverent, at this shrine to modernity,
dreaming of the highways soon to be,
cities rising where trees now stand.

Dragon's-Blood Trees

—after Beth Moon, *Heart of the Dragon*

In a dream they appear to me,
upright as shaving brushes,
the dragon's-blood trees
of Socotra Island, off the Horn
of Africa, silver as shadows,
exposing their undersides, a tangle
of arterial branches like the gills
of gigantic mushrooms or the intricate
crinoline skirts of girls tumbling
immodestly onto the grass.
Expecting sentient if sessile beings,
I address them, but being
as earth-bound as I am, they
do not respond. To the Socotrans,
these trees seem as ordinary as oaks
common as a cabbage white.
Yet they know the power of the trees'
thick red sap, harvesting from this
a medicine and dye too useful
for the trees' own good.

Sea Bed

—after Leio McLaren

The sea spreads her lacy
petticoats wide on the dunes,
dry as dusty animals
grazing in the field.
Over and over, she licks
their flanks till they
disappear. From above,
from the view of a pelican
hovering over a trawler,
we can see the tide
rise, sweeping off every
shed shell polished by the shifting
of wind and water. And here,
so small we hardly notice,
a woman sleeps
on her pillow of sand.
She doesn't sense
the surf coming closer
till it almost touches
her curved instep, like
a blanket she has
tossed aside. It goes on
hollowing the dunes with its
subtle blades, casting up
thick tangles of kelp,
driftwood bouquets.

Family Portrait, With Weapons

—after Oceola Refetoff, *Bruce and Elsie,*
Independence, CA

In this place, nothing grows
but tumbleweed backed up
to the blue hills. To thrive here,
creatures must tunnel underground,
possess protective thorns or venom.
Yet this couple's plump, contented.
They love the desert's thrifty blessings,
its arid silences. In another age,
she might bake casseroles or knit.
He'd take up whittling or the fiddle,
hunting only for subsistence. Now
killing has become a way of life.
Rifles slung astride their shoulders,
they walk out of a morning.
Bullets nesting in the chambers
herald their presence, power
over everything that lives.

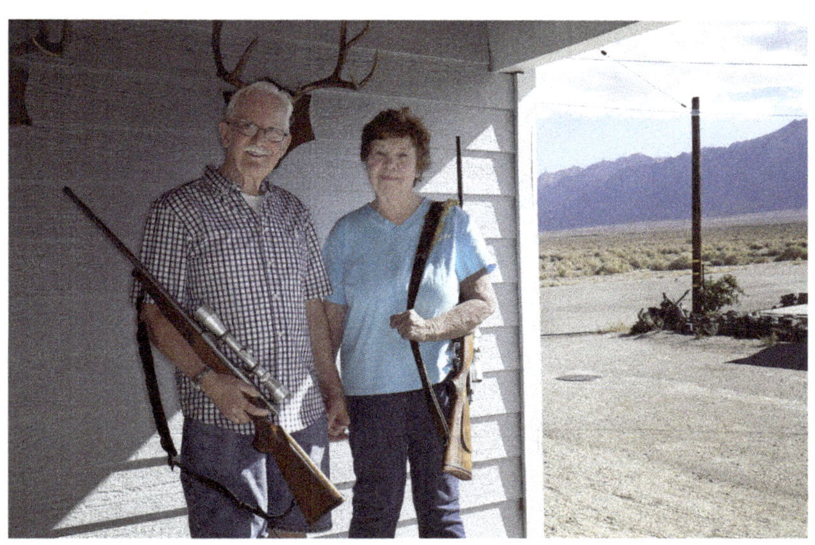

Oceola Refetoff, *Bruce and Elsie, Independence, CA*

Ghost Wall

—after Suzanne Simmons, *Trespass*

Trees are patient, setting seed,
persisting silently. They know
what holds is what's beneath.
The roots keep spreading,
exposing veins of rebar.
At last, weather and the years
bring down the wall, insisting
this place belongs to no one.
Where the wall once was,
a stand of slender sycamores
hoist tangled branches,
rooting out the vestiges,
asserting their dominion.

Pearblossom

—after David Hockney, *Pearblossom Highway*

Composed as any nature morte,
the highway, built block by photographic
block, extends to the horizon, beyond,
yet perversely commands us to halt,
though in life, we would surely
speed through this empty stretch,
miles from any enforcement.
Insistent Joshua trees gesture
like martyrs at the side of the road,
eager for escape, as the desert
erases the asphalt,
turning it back to sand.

Under the Metal

—after Daniel Mauermann, *Pierced Man*

My father used to have a piece of ground—mostly
patchy crabgrass, with a few surprises poking
through the tangle of dead stalks – clouds of Mariposa
orchids, hibiscus, wide as my open palm, and roses.
He'd stand there, watching it all grow. That's how
my piercings started. I had only this brown body.
I'd watch the big dudes running at the track, tattoos
on every patch of naked skin. Their muscles rippled,
making wind blow through the roses climbing up
their arms. I loved their power. But ink doesn't really
change you. Metal, though, might make a person
more than just himself. With enough bolts and screws,
sharp skewers, I'd be invincible. That's why I lined
those spikes up on my cheeks. And the beads?
Before Columbus and his crew landed their ships
on alien soil, my ancestors would carve designs
into their faces, layer on some river mud, make
themselves as beautiful as birds, their naked bodies
gleaming in the sun. It scared the crap out of the
Europeans. I've lost my tribe. These piercings
may not make me beautiful, but people see me.
They ask How long did it take to get like that?
Did it hurt? How do you keep from catching all
those metal rings on shirts? I ask myself what
I will do when all the skin on my face and neck
runs out. Already, the only open space is on
my scalp. When there's no more room
for piercings, who will I be?

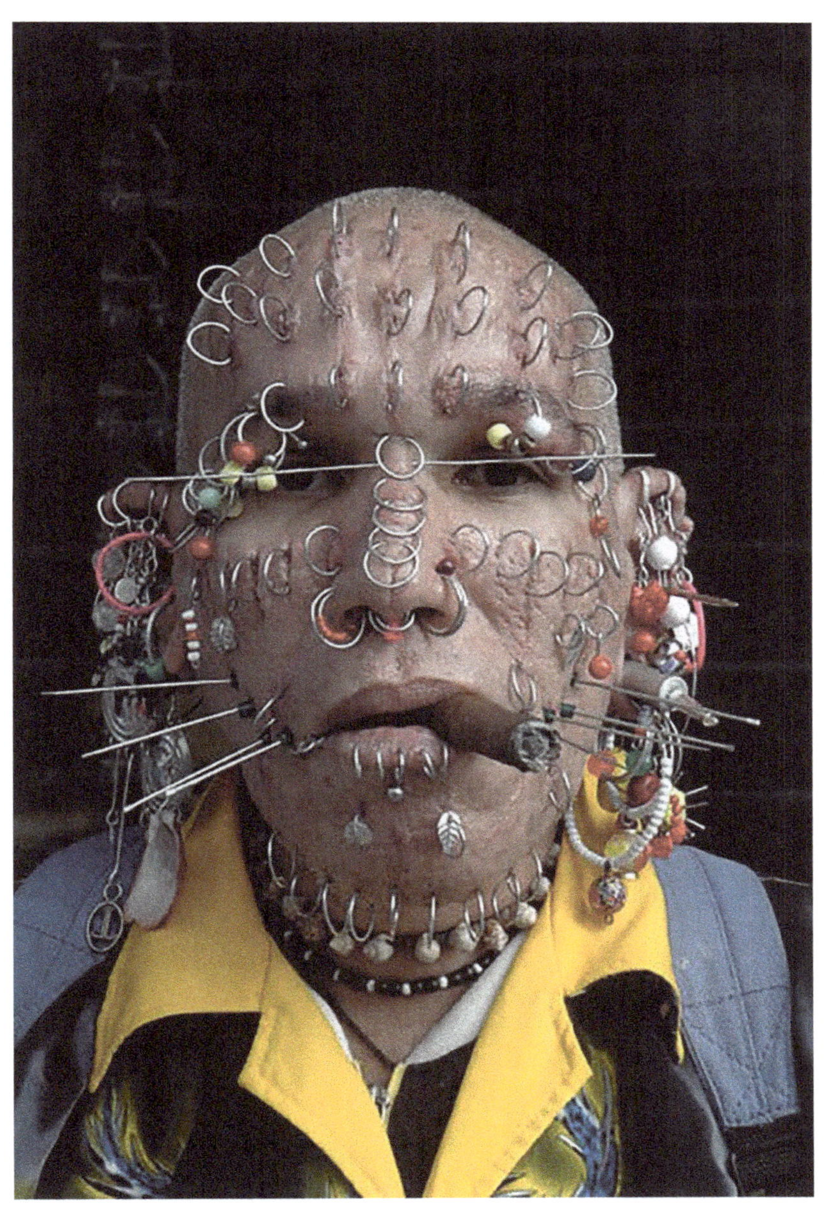

Daniel Mauermann, *Pierced Man*, 2008

Man Smoking

—after Josef Capek, *Piják*

He was fleshy as a toadstool, blonde and plump,
loved his brandy, lived in a well-appointed
suite with many windows. One day, he slung
a gun over his shoulders, went to war.
When he returned, his eyes shifted like birds
starting at loud sounds. He sold his furniture,
moved to a town where he knew no one.
Renting a narrow set of rooms, all angles,
he took up absinthe and cheap cigars.
Soon, his ruddy hue had faded to a yellow
outline, bright as police tape marking
the site of accidents or violent crimes.
A demolished house, haunt of broken
bannisters, sagging wallpaper, he
collapsed in on himself, skin the blue
of fog over a swamp. One day, the gun
spoke out one loud last word. A wisp
of smoke rose in the blue room.
Then he was gone, just gone.

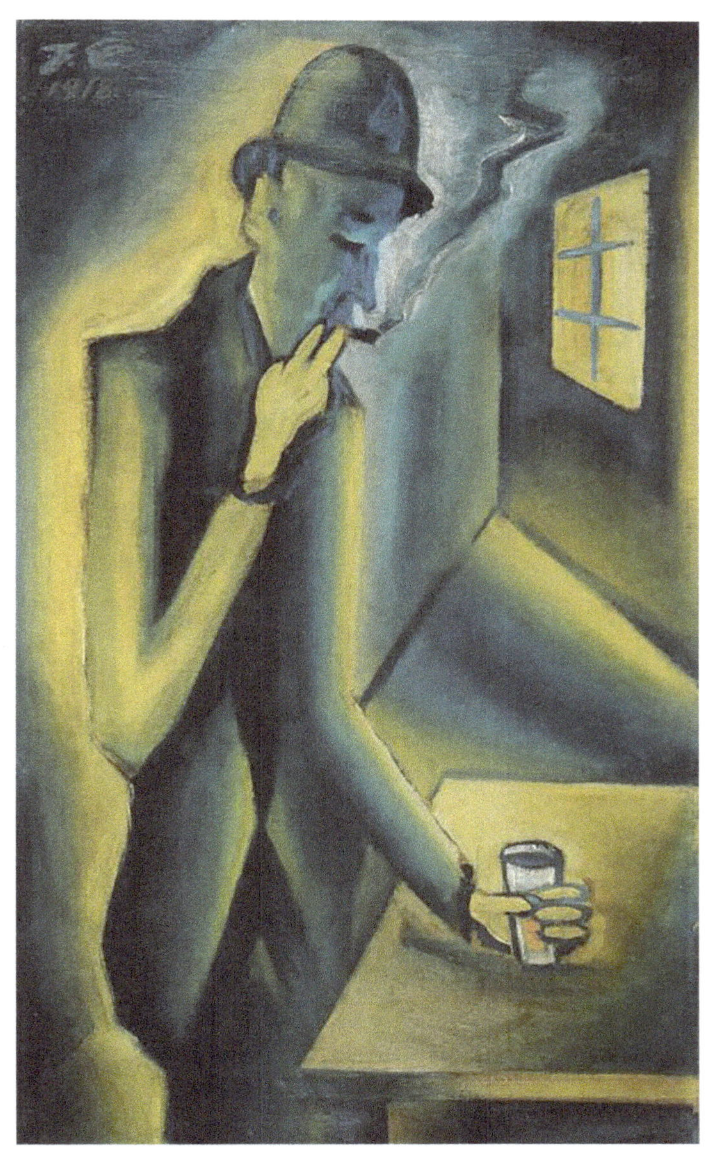

Josef Capek, *Piják*, 1918–19

Ark

After summer burned it all down to the ground,
we started bringing outdoors in, soft sheep's wool,
sand transmuted into glass, wood, planed smooth
and fashioned into furniture. Out there, so much
has disappeared. Once, every flower housed
its multitude of bees, and tiny hermit crabs
explored the shore. They're gone now.
We're building a museum of lost elements
so no one forgets the way things used to be.
Outside, gray sky broods, rainclouds spilling over.
But except for the narrow strip of splattered
pane, the sound of wind, we hardly know it.
We've been layering the patterns as a bird
constructs a nest, lined with soft down,
one twig at a time. A puzzle sky, complete
with birds, vying at a feeder. Just a few
more bits to add, and then we'll have it.
The braided rug and chairs take their color
(chili red) from the hollyhocks that used to
grow beside the gate. When the puzzle's done,
the painting framed, brushes soaking in a jar
of turpentine, when wave-patterned shades
have been pulled tight, and rain turns into
snow, we'll wonder—when we open up
the door, will we be stranded on a rock,
adrift on a gray sea of clouds, left all alone?

The Wall

—after Debbie McAfee

Clouds easily evade barbed wire.
Citizens of sky, we spurn your sorry efforts
to shut a people in or out, to set a border.
Subject only to the weather, we
sail above you, understand solidity
as an illusion. In time,
wire rusts. Wood grows porous,
stone swells and contracts
so often it reverts
to sand.
The roots of plants,
rivers' changing courses,
the tunneling of animals
and others
all thwart the wall.
Your barriers
are policy.
To break
their bonds is
natural law.
Everything
conspires against
your flimsy
empire.

Bridal Salon

After the bombs fell, vestiges remained for a long while,
but there was no one to collect them, no children to listen
to old tales about the world before; no adults to tell them.
Not even rats to gnaw these dresses to white shreds.
They might as well be stone, marble-white as statues
in the ruins of Pompei or Rome. But the sun still goes on
rising, light still keeps pouring through the narrow window,
gilding the gowns' rich taffeta and silk, embroidered trains.
The veils' white froth flows like surf across the floor, holding
shards of brittle moonlight in its folds. How long has it been
since bombs rained down, leaving property intact but
    destroying
every living thing? Time stopped when the last eye ceased
    to perceive it.

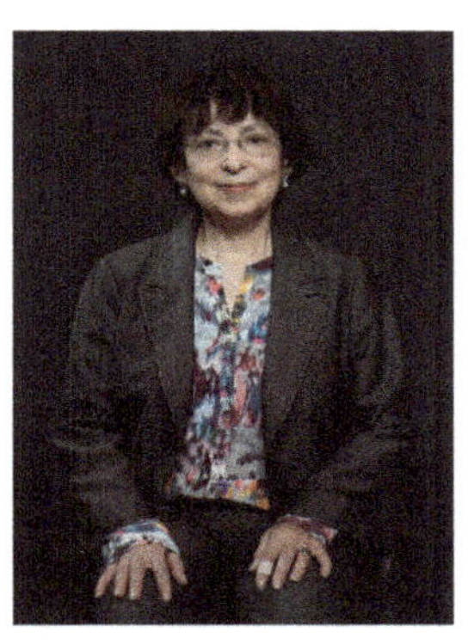

ROBBI NESTER is the author of five books of poetry and editor of three ekphrastic anthologies. A retired college educator, she currently hosts and curates two poetry series on Zoom. Learn more at her website: www.robbinester.net.

SHANTI ARTS

NATURE ▪ ART ▪ SPIRIT

Please visit us online
to browse our entire book catalog,
including poetry collections and fiction,
books on travel, nature, healing, art,
photography, and more.

Also take a look at our highly regarded art
and literary journal, *Still Point Arts Quarterly*,
which may be downloaded for free.

www.shantiarts.com